# MEDITATIONS

## ON THE

## INSATIABLE

## SOUL

## BY ROBERT BLY

*Poetry*
Silence in the Snowy Fields
The Light Around the Body
Sleepers Joining Hands
Jumping Out of Bed
This Tree Will Be Here for a Thousand Years
The Man in the Black Coat Turns
Loving a Woman in Two Worlds
Selected Poems

*Prose Poems*
The Morning Glory
This Body Is Made of Camphor and Gopherwood
What Have I Ever Lost by Dying?

*Prose*
The Eight Stages of Translation
A Little Book on the Human Shadow
American Poetry: *Wildness and Domesticity*
Iron John: *A Book About Men*
Remembering James Wright

*Translations*
The Story of Gösta Berling by Selma Lagerlöf
Hunger by Knut Hamsun
Twenty Poems of Georg Trakl
Neruda and Vallejo: *Selected Poems*
Lorca and Jimenez: *Selected Poems*
Friends: You Drank Some Darkness
*Three Swedish Poets: Martinson, Ekelöf, and Tranströmer*
The Kabir Book: *44 of the Ecstatic Poems of Kabir*
Twenty Poems of Rolf Jacobsen
Twenty Poems of Vincente Aleixandre *(with Lewis Hyde)*
Selected Poems of Rainer Maria Rilke
Time Alone: *Selected Poems of Antonio Machado*
Twenty Poems of Olav H. Hauge
Ten Poems of Francis Ponge Translated by Robert Bly and
Ten Poems of Robert Bly Inspired by the Poems of Francis Ponge

*Editor*
Leaping Poetry
The Sea and the Honeycomb: *80 Tiny Poems*
News of the Universe: *Poems of Twofold Consciousness*
Forty Poems Touching on Recent American History
A Poetry Reading Against the Vietnam War
The Winged Life: *Selected Poems and Prose of Thoreau*
The Rag and Bone Shop of the Heart: *An Anthology*
(with James Hillman and Michael Meade)
The Darkness Around Us Is Deep: *Selected Poems of William Stafford*

*Interviews*
Talking All Morning: *Collected Interviews and Conversations*

*For Pierre*

# MEDITATIONS ON THE INSATIABLE SOUL

*asa gift*  *from Joan*

POEMS

BY

# ROBERT BLY

HarperPerennial

*A Division of* HarperCollins*Publishers*

HarperCollins books may be purchased for educational, business, or sales promotional use. For information please write: Special Markets Department, HarperCollins Publishers, Inc., 10 East 53rd Street, New York, NY 10022.

FIRST EDITION

*Designed by Alma Hochhauser Orenstein*

Library of Congress Cataloging-in-Publication Data

Bly, Robert.
    Meditations on the insatiable soul : poems / by
Robert Bly. — 1st ed.
      p.  cm.
    ISBN 0-06-055357-X/ISBN 0-06-095063-3 (pbk.)
    I. Title.
PS3552.L9S65   1994        93-41009
811'.54—dc20

94 95 96 97 98 DT/RRD 10 9 8 7 6 5 4 3 2 1
94 95 96 97 98 DT/RRD 10 9 8 7 6 5 4 3 2 1 (pbk.)

# Contents

## THREE

## FOUR

# ONE

# Men and Women

♦ 1 ♦

Horses go on eating the Apostle Island ferns,
Also sheep and goats; also the big-nostriled moose
Who knocks down the common bushes
In his longing for earthly pleasure.
The moose's great cock floats in the lily pads.
That image calms us. His nose calms us.
Slowly, obstinately, we retrieve the pleasures
The Fathers, angry with the Gnostics, threw away.

♦ 2 ♦

The glad body sings its four-leggéd tunes.
It has its honesty. Lovers know the obstinacy
Of the hippopotamus, the grunts that say to spirit,
Gone, gone. The lover's body leaps at its own
Sweetness, snaps off blossoms with its teeth. Later

3

He seems good to her eyes, like a waterhole
Muddied by animals. Tristan and Isolde
Love their bawdy lodge, no north, no south.

◆ 3 ◆

Men wrong women, because a woman wants the
    two things
Joined, but the man wants sawn boards,
He wants roads diverging, and jackdaws flying,
Heaven and earth parted. Women wrong men,
Because the woman wants doves returning at dusk,
Clothes folded, and giants sitting down at table.
One wants an eternal river—which one? And the
    other wants
A river that makes its own way to the ocean.

# Waiting for the Stars

◆ 1 ◆

How much I long for the night to come
Again—I am restless all afternoon—
And the huge stars to appear
All over the heavens!—The black spaces between
     stars—
And the blue to fade away.

◆ 2 ◆

I worked on things with my back to the window,
Waiting for the darkness that I remember
I saw from my cradle.
When I step over and open the door, I am
A salmon slipping over the gravel into the ocean.

One star stands alone in the western darkness:
Arcturus. Caught in their love, the Arabs called it
The Keeper of Heaven. I think
It was in the womb that I received
The thirst for the dark heavens.

# The Man Who Walks Toward Us

There is so much forgotten rock in the world
And so much blue, glacial ice crowding down to
    die,
So many overhangs on which no petroglyphs are
    ever found,
And so many ships that rise up and slip down with
    no iceberg near.

There are stories long told that have never been
    understood
And so many metaphors that Valentinus muttered
    to the frogs
And so much wainscoting that widows have
    painted over.
There are moments when the gold sun in Lisbon is
    gone.

We see houses in our dreams that need to be
    repaired
And horses that no one has fed for three weeks.
There are so many shoulders we have never
    touched with our fingers,
And there are days when I forget I have a mother.

We drink down so many angers at our mother's
    breast.
There are so many cries no one makes during the
    wedding service.
There are so many poets whose poems no one
    reads
And so many pale bottles that the demons set out
    for milk.

Certain streams go into a mountain and never come
    out again.
Boys ride rafts down that dark tunnel, we mustn't
    wait for them.
Sometimes a twin lives with us in the womb for a
    while and then vanishes at birth.
There is a man who walks toward us for days, for
    years, for sixty years

And arrives, opens the bed clothes, sleeps with us
    until dawn,
Leaving behind a piece of ivory from the narwhal's
    horn, pierced with many holes.

# The Chinese Peaks

*For Donald Hall*

I love the mountain peak
but I know also its rolling
foothills
half-invisible
in mist and fog.

The Seafarer gets up
long before dawn to read.
His soul
is a whale feeding
on the Holy Word.

The soul who loves the peak
also inhales the deep
breath rising
from the mountain
buried in mist.

# Letter to James Wright

My dear James, do you know that nothing has
    happened
Since you died? Ammons is still writing garbage,
And the *Maximus Poems* are back in print. *"Well, I*
    *am tired*
*Of the lost maples of heaven; I want news*
*Of the living, of you."* Rexroth is gone. He was one
    of the
Funniest men in the world, and he got a biographer
With no sense of humor. *"I remember Rexroth saying,*
*'I'll cold-cock Santa Claus if he comes near.' It's the least*
*An anarchist can do. Eisenhower couldn't find*
*The Brazilian flag if it were up his butt."* Roger Hecht
    died
Along with Morgan Blum; Kenyon fumbled your
    papers

And lost them; they've named a street after you
In Martins Ferry. *"Do you remember that cliff*
*We once imagined—hundreds of swallow holes,*
*And an old Chinese poem rolled up inside*
*Each hole? We can't unroll them here. We have*
*To climb inside."* Even butterflies unfold. . . .
*"That tenderness . . . By God, I'll try anything."*

## Wallace Stevens and Florence

Oh Wallace Stevens, dear friend,
You are such a pest. You are so sure.
You think everyone is in your family.

It is you and your father and Mozart—
And ladies tasting cold rain in Florence,
Puzzling out inscriptions, studying the gold flake.

It is as if life were a visit to Florence,
A place where there are no maggots in the flesh,
No one screaming, no one afraid.

Your job, your joy, your morning walk,
As if you walked on the wire of the mind,
High above the elephants; you cry out a little but
    never fall.

As if we could walk always high above the world,
No bears, no witches, no Macbeth,
No one screaming, no one in pain, no one afraid.

# On the Oregon Coast

*For William Stafford*

The waves come—the large fourth wave
Looming up, thinking, crashing down—all
Roll in so prominently that I become small
And write this in a cramped script, hard to read.

Well, all this fury, prominent or not
Is also hard to read, and the ducks don't help,
Settling down in furry water, shaking
Themselves, and then forgetting it within a
        minute.

Remembering the fury, it is up to us, even
Though we feel small compared to the loose
Ocean, to keep sailing and not land,
And figure out what to say to our children.

# When William Stafford Died

Well, water goes down the Montana gullies.
"I'll just go around this rock and think
About it later." That's what you said.
When death came, you said, "I'll go there."

There's no sign you'll come back. Sometimes
My father sat up in the coffin and was alive again.
But I think you were born before my father,
And the feet they made in your time were lighter.

One dusk you were gone. Sometimes a fallen tree
Holds onto a rock, if the current is strong.
I won't say my father did that, but I won't
Say he didn't either. I was watching you both.

If all a man does is to watch from the shore,
Then he doesn't have to worry about the current.
But if affection has put us into the stream,
Then we have to agree to where the water goes.

# Thomas and the Codfish's Psalm

• 1 •

*The Gaiety of Form*

How sweet to weight the line with all these vowels!
Body, Thomas, the codfish's psalm. The gaiety
Of form lies in the labor of its playfulness.
The chosen vowel reappears like the evening star
Westerly, in the solemn return the astronomers
    love.
It comforts us, says: "I am here, be calm."
When a vowel returns three times, then it becomes
A note; and the whole stanza turns to music.

• 2 •

*The Turtle's Work*

Climbing on shore to give her brood a home,
The turtle gathers each day bits of primitive hay,
Piling her leathery eggs at pale midnight.

18

Obedient to some other moon, to her longing
And the night, her claws bury the eggs
Gleaming in the moonlight, cover them with sand.
Though she cannot protect them from the gulls on
    shore,
Some young find their way to the enormous sea.

# Honoring Sand

*In memory of Joseph Campbell*

We know the road the gods take, but we do not
    know
Who will walk on it. All moves slowly
In the soul. There is so much time
We can stay in grieving another hundred years.
The first harp came from an empty turtle.
The ocean thistle that has given up its flowering
Stays there, and its stem teaches us to go down.
Forget the flower; learn to know the sand.

# Gratitude to Old Teachers

When we stride or stroll across the frozen lake,
We place our feet where they have never been.
We walk upon the unwalked. But we are uneasy.
Who is down there but our old teachers?

Water that once could take no human
     weight—
We were students then—holds up our feet,
And goes on ahead of us for a mile.
Beneath us the teachers, and around us the
     stillness.

# Thoughts in the Cabin

Why do I suddenly feel free of panic?
Here a summer afternoon, wind-
Blown lake, a cabin of strong logs.

I can live and die with no more
Fame; I'd like ground to walk on,
A few books, occasionally a storm.

I know stories I can tell, and I may
Or may not. There is more
To learn: the wind and the screendoor.

The granary of images, the Norwegian
Lore, the power of Schmad Razum,
Good or evil, success or failure.

Expect something else from me—
Less—and don't rule out
Misdirection, silence, misinformation.

# Two

# The Spiny Beast

My father and I
Swim a half-mile
Or so apart
In a cold sea.
We are each aware
Of the other's strokes, but,
We swim far from
The care of women.
I swim on, asking
My shoulders why
My lower half
Feels so heavy.
Only my arms
Lift, the ocean
Pulls the rest
Of me down.

I know that far
Below us, scattered
On the ocean floor, are
Model A engines,
Spoked wheels
From horse rakes,
Engine blocks
Broken apart,
Cutting bars, snapped
Ploughshares,
Drive-shafts
Sticking from sand,
Thresher pulleys.
Our failures
Have solidified
There, rusting
In saline water.
We worked all day
Through dinner till
Midnight and couldn't
Keep the swather
Going, nothing helps,
Drove a piston
Right through the block.
It won't do.
And behind us
A large beast
Swims—four or

Five miles back,
Spines on his nose,
Fins like the
Komodo dragon,
Spiny whiskers,
Following us.

# My Father at Eighty-Five

His large ears
Hear everything.
A hermit wakes
And sleeps in a hut
Underneath
His gaunt cheeks.
His eyes blue, alert,
Disappointed,
And suspicious,
Complain I
Do not bring him
The same sort of
Jokes the nurses
Do. He is a bird
Waiting to be fed,—
Mostly beak—an eagle

Or a vulture, or
The Pharaoh's servant
Just before death.
My arm on the bedrail
Rests there, relaxed,
With new love. All
I know of the Troubadours
I bring to this bed.
I do not want
Or need to be shamed
By him any longer.
The general of shame
Has discharged
Him, and left him
In this small provincial
Egyptian town.
If I do not wish
To shame him, then
Why not love him?
His long hands,
Large, veined,
Capable, can still
Retain hold of what
He wanted. But
Is that what he
Desired? Some
Powerful engine
Of desire goes on

Turning inside his body.
He never phrased
What he desired,
And I am
His son.

# My Father's Neck

Your chest, hospital gown
Awry, looks
Girlish today.
It is your bluish
Reptile neck
That has known weather.
I said to you, "Are
You ready to die?"
"I am," you said,
"It's too boring
Around here." He has in mind
Some other place
Less boring. "He's
Not ready to go,"
The Doctor said.
There must have been

A fire that nearly
Blew out, or a large
Soul, inadequately
Feathered, that became
Cold and angered.
Some four-year-old boy
In you, chilled by your
Mother, misprized
By your father, said,
"I will defy, I will
Win anyway, I
Will show *them*."
When Alice's well-
Off sister offered to
Take your two boys
During the Depression,
You said it again.
Now you bring that
Defiance to death.
This four-year-old
Old man in you does as
He likes: he likes
To stay alive.
Through him you
Get revenge,
Persist, endure,
Overlive, overwhelm,
Get on top.

You gave me
This, and I do
Not refuse it.
It is
In me.

# Sitting with My Mother and Father

My father's hard breathing
We all three
Notice. To continue
To live here,
He must take air.
But taking air
Commits him
To sharing it
With wolves and cattle.
When breathing stops,
He will be free
Of that company.
He came from the water
World, and does not
Want to change
Again.

My mother is not sure
Where she wants
To be, but this air
World is all she can
Remember, and nieces
Are here, nephews,
Classmates, a son.
She sits with puzzled eyes,
As if to say,
"Where is
That reckless man
For whom I gladly left
My father?
Is it this man
With gaunt cheeks
On the bed?
All those times
I drove into town,
Carefully, over packed
Snow, is this
What it comes to?" Yes,
It is, my dear
Mother.
The tablecloths
You saved
Are all gone;
The baked corn dish
You made for your boys,

The Christmas Eves,
Opening perfume—
*Evening in Paris*—
From your husband,
The hope that a man
Would alter his habits
For you—
They are all gone.
The nurse takes my father
For his bath.
You and I
Wait here
For Jacob to come
Back.
"What sort
Of flowers are those?"
"Daisies," I say.
A few minutes
Later you ask
Again.
What can I
Do but feel
Time
Go through me,
And sit here
With you?

# To My Mother

What can we say
To each other?
That we are nothing
When the Man
Leaves the room?
That each of us is bound
By our breathing
To this troubled place?
That I am a son,
And you a mother,
And that someone
Has come between
Us, so that we
Forget
What has saved us?

# The Threshing Machine

You are eighty-
Six, and, while we
Talk, suddenly
Fall asleep.
Would you have been
Proud of me
If I had lived
More like you?
In this same hospital
Room, as you were
Drying out thirty-five
Years ago, you asked:
"Are you happy?"
I was twenty-eight.
"Happiness is not one

Of the aims I have
Set for my life."
You were alarmed.
I was bluffing, as
Isolated as you.
Now you have almost reached
The last station.
Shall I say that you
Misspent your life?
You stood vibrating
On a threshing machine,
Pulleys, choppers, shakers
Below you,
And kept your balance
Mostly.
I walked on a shaky rope,
Carrying six
Children on my shoulders,
Felt their love.
A woman whom I knew
From the ocean had
A message for me
And it arrived.
Now for the first time
I can see your skull
Below your closed
Grape-like eyes.

Some modest,
Luminous
Thing has happened.
What more
Did we expect?

# Prayer for My Father

Your head is still
Restless, rolling
East and west.
That body in you
Insisting on living
Is the old hawk
For whom the world
Darkens.
If I am not
With you when you die,
That is grievous
But just.
That part of you
Cleaned my bones more
Than once. But I
Will meet you

In the young hawk
Whom I see
Inside both
You and me. He
Will guide you
To the Lord of Night,
Who will give you
The tenderness
You wanted here.

# Dream of Myself at Twelve

At the start of the dream
It was understood you were working
In the grape fields. But
When I walked
Into the barn, I saw

A leg sticking
From the hay. It was you, hiding,
Not working. "How
Long have you
Been here?" Your head

Rose from the hay.
My mother, your calm wife,
Showed up, spoke
For you, said,
"Jacob, you haven't been

Drinking, have you?"
How often as a child I heard
That and did nothing.
This time I broke
A horse-collar, threw

A gun into
The horse-stall, jabbed
A pitchfork into
Loose hay,
Hit the hired man.

My father said nothing.
My brother said it was clear
I could never be-
Come a man,
Would have to play with toys.

Then I looked
Down to the yellow straw
In the stable, my tongue
Still. As I
Woke, a small boy

Clung to me,
Could not feel safe,
Would not take
His arms
From around my neck.

# Having Time At Last

How wild your eyes were
When I saw them last!
The chair steadied
Your back, but your head
Bobbed wild as a bird's,
About to feed. Your eyes pleaded,
Without their usual need
To dominate. You must have
Seen some tree out the window,
The wind-blown leaves falling.

Now those eyes have closed.
Do we have time at last
For each other now? Do
You have time for me?
What good was all that careful

Seeing we did, to miss
Pheasant nests as we mowed,
Or rocks as we plowed?
Eyes, we both found out,
Are also for weeping.

I place my hand on your chest.
Your chest is thin
Below the burial suit,
A chicken's breast
Below my hand.
Do you feel I glory
In my power as I lay
My hand on your chest?
A voice says to me:
"For now you are the standing one. . . ."

# A Dream of the Blacksmith's Room

◆ 1 ◆

I was teaching when you died.
The coffin lid
Lifted shows some
Fall oakleaves sewn
High above
Your winter face.

How strange it is that I have
Leisure near
Your cream-colored hands.
I write down what you did,
Or did wrong, or did
Not do at all.

The funeral director, a kind
Man, says, "I'll

Leave and go upstairs
With my family. You sit as long
As you like.
No one is here."


♦ 2 ♦

Your marriage held in-
Visible mountains, touching
And not touching . . .
Too much isolation. I'm not sure
You married at all,
Or whom you married.


For twenty-five years,
An adult, I lived
A half-mile from you.
Why? Perhaps I couldn't get
Enough, or perhaps
I was your wife.


Already twenty-eight
By that time,
When I moved back,
I wanted to be a hermit,
"Take no part,"
Live alone,

Be called away by
Wind, build
A house of one room,
Live there, be silent
As a blade of grass,
Have no woman.

Weren't you my husband?
A hurtful man,
Reckless, wrathful, solemn,
Able to break a man or a book,
Gentle, un-
Churched, bold.

We had twenty-four
Anniversaries then,
Before I moved again,
At fifty-three,
No longer needing
To be married to you.

As I wrote that down, your head
Turned slowly
In the coffin, your jaw
Opened, the teeth showed
Themselves; then
Your head rolled back.

I dreamt last night you
Lived near me, not
Dead at all, safe,
In a blacksmith's storage room,
Screws and bolts in bins
From floor to ceiling.

You visited, brought me
An ivory jar,
Holding some precious fluid,
Which I took. I knew it meant
A crisis had come
But I let you leave.

Later, the door opened,
A man threw
Your body down, a wizened,
Astonishingly small body,
Rope still tied
Around the neck.

I cried out to my wife,
"He didn't die
That way!" The man who threw
The body said, "It's over. You
Don't have to
Rescue him again."

# THREE

# Meditations on the Insatiable Soul

The man who sits up late at night cutting
His nails, the backs of black whales, the tip
Of the mink's tail, the tongue that slips out of lips,
    all of these
Testify to a soul used to eating and being eaten.
Urged on by the inner pressure of teeth,
Some force, animal-born, is slippery, edgy,
Impatient, greedy to pray for new heavens,
Unforgiving, resentful, like a fire in dry wood.

Greeks sit by the fire cleaning their bright teeth.
Let Portia grieve in her sorrowing house.
Let blackbirds come. The insatiable soul
Begins to eat shellfish, the Caribbean islands,

The rainforests, Amazon. Who wants to eat the
    meat
Cooked in the Holocaust? Oh, you know.
The traveler asleep in Charlemagne's cave
Laughs in his murky unshaven dream.


◆ 3 ◆

Some ill-smelling, libidinous, worm-shouldered
Deep-reaching desirousness rules the countryside.
Let sympathy pass, a stranger, to other shores!
Let the love between men and women be ground
    up
And fed to the talk shows! Let every female breast
Be photographed! Let the father be hated! Let the
    son be hated!
Let twelve-year-olds kill the twelve-year-olds!
The Great Lord of Desirousness ruling all.


◆ 4 ◆

Northern lights illumine the storm-troll's house.
There men murdered by God promenade.
The buffalo woman plays her bony flute calling
The lonely father trampled by the buffalo god.
The foreskins of angels shelter the naked cradle.

The stew of discontents feeds the loose souls.
And the owl husbands the moors, harries the
    mouse,
Beforehand, behindhand, with his handsome eyes.

# Anger Against Children

The vet screams, and throws his crutch at a
    passerby.
"Hey, lady, you want to meet a child-killer?"
African drums play all night for the women
With their heads down on motel tables.
Parents take their children into the deepest Oregon
    forests,
And leave them there. When the children
Open the lunchbox, there are stones inside, and a
    note saying, "Do your own thing."
And what would the children do if they found their
    way home in the moonlight?
The planes have already landed on Maui, the
    parents are on vacation.
Our children live with a fear at school and in the
    house.

The mother and father do not protect the younger
    child from the savagery of the others.
Parents don't want to face the children's rage,
Because the parents are also in rage.


What is it like to have stayed this long in
    civilization—
To have witnessed the grave of Tutankhamen open
    once more—
What is it like to wear sweatshirts and bluejeans
And wait for hours to see the bracelets of those
    wasteful death-coddlers,
Who learned to conquer conscious life?
What is it like to have the dynamo, the lightbulb,
    the Parliamentary system,
    the electrical slaves embedded in
    elevator doors,
The body scanners that see sideways, the
    extravagant and elegant fighters,
And still be unconscious? What is that like?


Well of course there is rage.
The thirty-four-year-old mother
Wants to reject the child still in the womb,
And she asks Senators to pass laws to prevent that.
The husband dreams of killing his wife, and the
    wife lays plots.
She imagines that he is an Oppressor,

And that she is an Aztec Princess.
In the night she holds an obsidian knife over her
husband's sleeping body.
He dreams he is a deer being torn apart by female
demons.


This is the rage that shouts at children.
This is the rage that cannot be satisfied,
Because each year more ancient Chinese art objects
go on display.
So the rage goes inward at last,
It ends in doubt, in self-doubt, dyeing the hair, and
love of celebrities.
The rage comes to rest at last in the talk show late
at night,
When the celebrities without anger or grief tell us
that only the famous are good, only they live
well.
There are waifs inside us, broken by the Pauline
gospels;
We know them,
And those who step on desire as a horse steps on
a chick.
No cry comes out, only silence, and the faint
whisper of the collapsing birdskull.


Here the sleepers sleep, here the Rams and the
Bears play.

The old woman weeps at night in her room at the
    Nursing Facility.
There are no bridges over the ocean.
She sees a short dock, and ahead of that darkness,
    hostile waters, lifting swells,
Fitfully lit, or not lit at all.
Tadpoles drowse in the stagnant holes.
The gecko goes back to his home in the cold rain.


The wife of the Chrysler dealer is in danger of being
    committed again.
She left the hospital hopeful, she struggles hard,
She reads Laing and Rollo May;
But nothing works, she dreams she is interred in
    Burma.
Cars go past her house at night, Japanese soldiers
    at the wheel.
Nothing can be done, the kernel opens, all is swept
    away;
She is carried out of sight.
The doctor arrives; once more she leaves dry-eyed
    for the hospital.


I am twenty-eight again. I sleep curled up,
My fingers widen as I sleep, my toes grow
    immense at night.
Tears flow; I am in some bin apart from him I love.

The ocean king, far at sea, lies alone on his bed.
His interior engine has been catapulted into
    fragments,
Valves and drive shaft scattered, the engine mount
    settles to sand.
The saddened king goes about, all night he reaches
    down,
Picking up bolts from the sand, and piston rings;
    by morning all is scattered again.

We wake, no dream is remembered, the scenes
    gone into smoke.
We are in some enormous place, abandoned,
Where Adam Kadmon has been forgotten, the
    luminous man is dissolved.
The sarcophagus contains the rotted bones of the
    monks; so many lived in the desert.
None are alive, only the bones lie in the dust.
My friend goes to Philadelphia to claim his father's
    body.
It lies in an uncarpeted room in the ghetto, there
    was no one else to claim the body.
The time of manifest destiny is over, the time of
    grief has come.

# FOUR

# St. George, the Dragon, and the Virgin

*A sculpture made by Bernt Notke*
*in 1489 for Stockholm Cathedral*

The spiny Dragon
Who lives in the rat-
Filled caves is losing.
He fights fiercely,
As when a child
Lifts his four
Feet to hold
Off the insane
Parent. The Dragon's
Hand grasps the wooden
Lance that has
Penetrated his thorny
Chest, but . . .
Too late. . . .

And this girlish knight?
Oh I know him.
I read the New
Testament as I lay
Naked on my bed
As a boy. The knight
Rises up radiant
With the forehead-
Eye that sees past
The criminal's gibbet
To the mindful
Towers of the spirit city.
I hate this solar
Boy whom I have been,
Rearing with his lance above
The father. Each of us
Has been this marsh
Dragon on his back.
He is Joseph, Grendel,
What we have forgotten,
The great spirit
The alchemists knew of,
Without whom is nothing.

How long it must've taken
To temper that horse
So he agreed
To abet the solar boy.

This earth-handed, disreputable,
Hoarse-voiced one
Is dying. As children
We knew ours
Was a muddy greatness.

Did I forget to mention
The Virgin? She prays
On her knees while
This goes on,
As well she might.

I wrote this to bless
The swamp monster
And the marsh hag
Who bore him.

## Ivar Oakeson's Fiddle

Let it be, let
It be. Let it be!
Portia awakes
In her sorrowing house;
The Orkney serpent
Lies close beside her,
Curls around her arm.

But the sorrowing fiddle
Has stayn awake all night.
The wooden-walled house
Is a resonating box.
The wood gourd that loves
The strings cries out
To those who love to dance.

Lovers and husbands
Whirl round and round.
Men and women
Sweat and shout, kick-
Ing and invit-
Ing their desire.
Oh, let it be.

# Question in the Los Gatos Hills

How often I have
Called to ponderable
Things: these
Eucalyptus-smelling
Sea-fogged
Hills
And chimney-hiding
Gorges;
I have called
Boulders to
Enter my poems,
Black dusty
Earth, rangy
Minnesota grass.
Why do I hesitate
Then to

Call to God?
Years ago I
Sat curled up
Behind a shed,
Saying to myself:
"You are a boy
Who will never
Be heard."
Forget that idea.
You are no
Longer a boy.
Let the sound come
Out of the mouth.
You hear the sitar
Cry, let the poem
Cry, even from
Behind the shed,
Where we all are.

# How David Did Not Care

What does it mean to live
As those before
Have lived? A field
Of boisterous men
And women who lift,
Shouting, singing,
And dancing a sheaf
Of wheat up to the sun.

When David danced for joy,
We guess he did not care.
When David played
The Song of Degrees
On his lute, when he cried,
"My bones call out
From the depths," then we know
He did not care.

For not to care is this:
To love the orphans
And the fatherless,
To dance as we sink
Into the badger's grief,
To let the resonating
Box of the body sound,
Not to ask to be loved.

# How the Saint Did Not Care

When we start westward
In Spain, we wander
Through vast expanses;
Among harsh gulleys
We find Roman leg-
Bones, Carthaginian
Spearheads, the bitter
Cross that betrayed so many.

When men and women lifted
The saint's body onto
A wagon, it was a lilac
Bush moving through
The French fields, so that
The reapers paused:
The fragrance shows how much
He did not care.

Who is it that can break
The hold the Cross has on
      us—
No not the Cross, the wolf
That eats up our desire.
Those who do not care
Retrieve one instant of time.
They dive as the cormorant
Dives after living fish.

# How Jonah Did Not Care

When have we had enough?
When we can turn our head,
Say no to the dog-headed,
Furry-nosed, anus-
Eyed beast of duty,
Give pay-back to God.
Friends, remember no one
Can see his own ears.

When Jonah sat
Shaded by the spindly
Leaves of a gourd,
Hot in the desert
Sand, he didn't care, nor
Did the worm who that night
Chewed the stalk
So that the gourd fell.

76

For not to care is this:
To love the sunlight,
As it falls on the table,
To leap out of misery
Once or twice
Like a great fish
Before falling
Back into the ocean.

# How Vincentine Did Not Care

A man bends over the gunwales,
Gazes into the sea
Hour after hour, sees
A lion rising upward.
If he looks to the sky, he sees
A dark egg perfectly
Visible in the Crow's
Stickly nest.

When the Terrible Nurse
Took Vincentine by the
Waist, and threw her
Into the ocean, a whale
Poured her into
His copious throat,
And there she lived
Without husband or children.

What does it matter,
Suffering or not!  Bad
Parents, or good
Parents, luck or none—
Let us agree to climb
The trunk of the Crow's tree,
And steal the Black
Egg from his nest!

# How Mirabai Did Not Care

My mother gave me body,
My father a black
Overcoat for the soul.
Now it is time to
Love the third power,
The black sun that shines
On bones and leaves
From beneath the earth.

Mirabai, night after night,
Let herself down castle
Walls on saris to visit
Her low-born teacher.
When she washed his old
Feet and drank the water,
Any idiot would know
She did not care.

Glimpsing the grave ahead,
The body leaps up, cries,
"What if it all ends!
What if the grave wins!"
Let it end—let the sand
And the ocean part,
Let it be, let
Heaven and earth go their ways.

## The Sun Crosses Heaven from West to East Bringing Samson Back to the Womb

Samson, grinding bread for widows and orphans,
Forgets he is wronged, and the answers
The Philistines wrangled out of him go back
Into the lion; the bitter and the sweet marry.
He himself wronged the lion. The burned wheat
Caresses the wind with its wifely tail; the jawbone
Runs in the long grass, and, having glimpsed
     heaven,
The fox's body saunters the tawny earth.

After death the soul returns to drinking milk
And honey in its sparse home. Broken lintels
Rejoin the sunrise gates, and bees sing
In sour meat. Once more in the cradle Samson's
Hair grows long and golden; Delilah's scissors

Turn back into two tiny and playful swords.
The sun, no longer haunted by sunset and
    shadows,
Sinks down in the Eastern ocean and is born.